ON-SCREEN ALIENS

DANNY PEARSON

Badger Publishing Limited
Oldmedow Road,
Hardwick Industrial Estate,
King's Lynn PE30 4JJ
Telephone: 01438 791037

www.badgerlearning.co.uk

8 10 9 7

On-Screen Aliens ISBN 978-1-78464-117-7

Text © Danny Pearson 2015

Complete work © Badger Publishing Limited 2015

All rights reserved. No part of this publication may be reproduced, stored in any form or by any means mechanical, electronic, recording or otherwise without the prior permission of the publisher.

The right of Danny Pearson to be identified as author of this work has been asserted by him in accordance with the Copyright, Designs and Patents Act 1988.

Publisher: Susan Ross
Senior Editor: Danny Pearson
Publishing Assistant: Claire Morgan
Designer: Fiona Grant
Series Consultant: Dee Reid

Photos: Cover Image: Science Photo Library/Alamy
Page 5: Geoff Moore/REX, WestEnd61/REX
Page 6: WestEnd61/REX
Page 7: Courtesy Everett Collection/REX
Page 8: SCIEPRO
Page 9: © World History Archive/Alamy
Page 10: Moviestore Collection/REX
Page 11: Courtesy Everett Collection/REX, Moviestore Collection/REX
Page 12: Moviestore Collection/REX
Page 13: Moviestore/REX
Page 14: Everett Collection/REX
Page 15: © AF archive/Alamy
Page 16: © Photos 12/Alamy, Paramount Pictures/courtesy/REX
Page 17: © Photos 12/Alamy
Page 18: © AF archive/Alamy
Page 19: H Lamb/Pwire/BEI/REX, © AF archive/Alamy
Page 20: © AF archive/Alamy
Page 21: © Moviestore collection Ltd/Alamy
Page 22: © AF archive/Alamy, © LFI/Photoshot
Page 23: Bonhams/Solent News/REX
Page 24: © ZUMA Press, Inc./Alamy
Page 25: Moviestore Collection/REX
Page 26: © AF archive/Alamy
Page 27: SNAP/REX
Page 28: © AF archive/Alamy
Page 29: c.20thC.Fox/Everett/REX
Page 30: © Worldspec/NASA/Alamy

Attempts to contact all copyright holders have been made.
If any omitted would care to contact Badger Learning, we will be happy to make appropriate arrangements.

ON-SCREEN ALIENS

Contents

1.	Are we alone?	5
2.	Weird aliens	9
3.	Then and now	14
4.	Alien spaceships	21
5.	Bringing aliens to life	24
	Questions	31
	Index	32

Badger LEARNING

Vocabulary

audiences   invisible
defeated   programmes
discovering   realistic
entertaining   released

1. ARE WE ALONE?

Could aliens have been on Earth before us?

Some people think so.

How else could there be strange statues found on Easter Island and huge unexplained lines in the Nazca desert of Peru?

WOW! facts

There are more than 70 different designs marked out onto the Nazca desert floor, which can only really be seen from the sky.

Many scientists believe that the universe is far too big for us to be alone in it.

Scientists are discovering faraway planets that could support life. They call these planets Goldilocks planets. This means they have conditions for life that are 'just right' to be able to live there.

So, are we alone in the universe?

Thousands of films and TV programmes have been made showing what people think aliens may look like.

One of the first films was a French film called *A Trip to the Moon*, made in 1902.

This film has aliens that look like strange lizard men. The humans that visit the Moon are captured by these aliens and they have to find a way to escape.

Special effects have moved on a lot since the first sci-fi films, but modern film-makers are still entertaining us with their weird and wonderful ideas of what aliens may look like.

2. WEIRD ALIENS

The War of the Worlds was written by an English author named H.G. Wells, in 1897.

In 1953, the book was made into a film.

The aliens in *The War of the Worlds* are from Mars and they almost win and take over Earth.

They are defeated at the very end by germs only found on this planet.

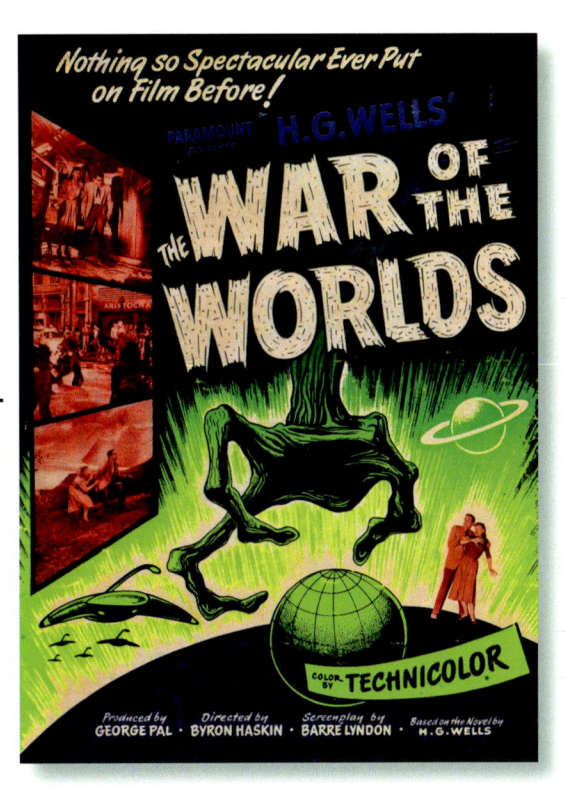

WOW! facts

A radio programme was made about *The War of the Worlds* in 1938. It was so realistic that listeners thought there was a real alien attack!

There were many alien films made during the 1950s and 60s. People loved to go to the cinema to be scared.

This very strange-looking alien is from the film *This Island Earth*, released in 1955.

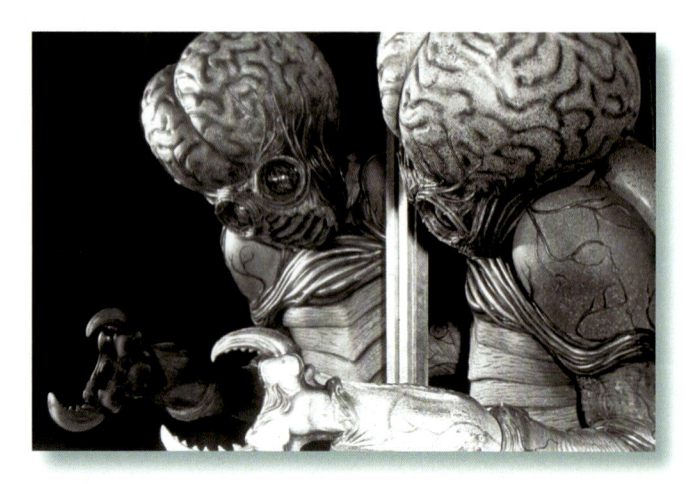

The Blob appeared in 1958. The blob crash-lands on Earth and it only grows bigger by eating humans.

It is eventually defeated by freezing it. The US Air Force pick the blob up and take it to the Arctic.

Little Shop of Horrors is a film about an alien plant that, like the blob, grows bigger by eating humans.

The film is a musical comedy rather than a horror film.

Mars Attacks is also a comedy sci-fi film. In the film, aliens kill off lots of people but are finally defeated when a boy finds out that the aliens' heads explode when they hear a certain song!

The Iron Giant is an animated film based on the book, *The Iron Man*, written by Ted Hughes.

The Iron Giant falls from space and is found by a young boy. The Iron Giant is a friendly alien but the army think he is some sort of weapon and try to destroy him.

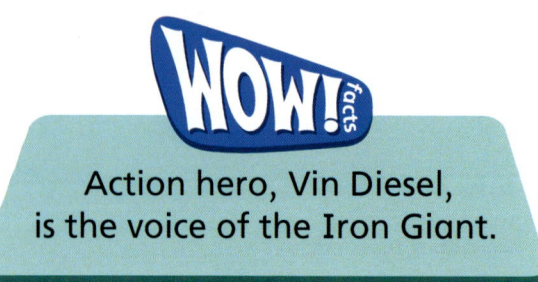

WOW! facts

Action hero, Vin Diesel, is the voice of the Iron Giant.

Marvel comics released the film *Guardians of the Galaxy* in 2014.

In it, a human named Peter Quill, or Star-Lord as he likes to be called, teams up with a gang of aliens to try and save the galaxy.

Star-Lord teams up with these aliens:
- Groot - strong, can change size, peaceful
- Rocket - expert with weapons, smart
- Drax the Destroyer - strong, fearless
- Gamora - quick, good fighter, smart

This group of misfits has proven so popular that a second film is being made.

3. THEN AND NOW

Some of the best aliens from film and TV have proven so popular that new films and programmes are still being made today.

Superman

Many people forget that Superman is, in fact, an alien. He was born on the planet Krypton. His parents placed him in a spaceship to escape from their exploding planet.

Superman first appeared on TV in 1951 and he then appeared on cinema screens in 1978.

The latest Superman film stars Henry Cavill.

In it, Superman will team up with Batman to fight evil here on Earth.

WOW! facts

The first Superman film won a Special Academy Award (an Oscar) for its special effects and was a huge hit in cinemas.

Star Trek has millions of fans. It started as a TV programme back in 1966.

Captain Kirk is the captain of the starship *Enterprise*. His second-in-command is Spock. He is one of the most famous aliens to appear on screen and has been played by two actors.

Leonard Nimoy was the first actor to play Spock.

Zachary Quinto plays Spock in the latest Star Trek films alongside the original Spock!

Spock's mother is human and his father is an alien called a Vulcan. Vulcans look very human, apart from having pointed ears.

Spock can knock someone out by pinching a nerve in their neck. Spock is also very clever and he likes to play 3D chess!

WOW! facts

Spock's skin was originally supposed to be red, but it didn't look right on camera.

The Star Wars films are some of the most popular films ever made.

The first film was made in 1979. Even though some characters such as Luke Skywalker and Han Solo look human, they are actually aliens.

Luke Skywalker's weapon is a lightsaber. The noise a lightsaber makes is created by combining the hum of an old TV and the buzz of a film projector's motor.

The Star Wars films have many different types of aliens and here are a few of the best:

- **Chewbacca** – a Wookie who flies with Han Solo on their spaceship the *Millennium Falcon*.

- **Yoda** – a Jedi Master who teaches Luke Skywalker the ways of the force in order to defeat his father, Darth Vader.

WOW! facts

In *The Phantom Menace*, Yoda has three toes. But in *The Empire Strikes Back*, *Return of the Jedi* and *Revenge of the Sith*, he has four.

- **Jabba the Hutt** – a criminal boss who wants to capture Han Solo.

- **Rancor** – Jabba the Hutt's pet that he keeps in his palace. The Rancoor is often used to eat Jabba's enemies.

4. ALIEN SPACESHIPS

Aliens on TV and in films not only look odd. They often have strange spaceships too.

In older films, aliens arrive on Earth in flying saucers. But as years have passed we have seen many different types of spaceship.

The Klingons, who appear in Star Trek, fly in a ship called a *Bird of Prey*. This ship can become invisible making the Klingons very hard to fight.

Han Solo and Chewbacca fly around space in a ship called the *Millennium Falcon*. They claim it is one of the fastest ships in the galaxy, although it often breaks down.

The alien ships that appear in the film *Independence Day* are the size of cities.

In one famous scene we can see one of the ships over the White House in Washington DC. It later goes on to destroy it.

The Tardis is used by Doctor Who to travel through space and time. It looks like an old police telephone box.

Tardis stands for:
Time **A**nd **R**elative **D**imension(s) **I**n **S**pace.

5. BRINGING ALIENS TO LIFE

There have been many tricks used to bring these aliens to life on film.

George Lucas, who directed four Star Wars films, asked the people who worked on The Muppet Show to help make a puppet to be Yoda.

What we see on screen in the original Star Wars trilogy is mostly a puppet.

WOW! facts

The voice of Yoda is spoken by the same man who voiced Fozzie Bear from *The Muppets*.

The Men in Black films also used puppets alongside computer effects to bring their characters to life.

Like the earlier sci-fi films, some of the aliens are actors in costumes. But, unlike the earlier films, the aliens in these films look very realistic.

Steven Spielberg has made some of the biggest and best-loved films of all time. Some of these have been about aliens.

His first famous alien film is called *Close Encounters of the Third Kind*, released in 1977.

In this film we are shown spaceships that are bigger than mountains.

In 1982, Spielberg released a film about an alien who gets stuck on Earth.

The alien makes friends with a boy and together they try to find a way of getting him back to his spaceship.

This film is called *E.T. the Extra-Terrestrial*.

E.T. is very strange-looking but he isn't scary. Maybe that is because he has big blue eyes?

Some people think he looks a bit like a cross between a pug dog and the famous scientist, Albert Einstein.

Spielberg got the idea of E.T. healing people by asking children what they thought E.T.'s powers should be.

James Cameron has made a few films involving aliens but his biggest alien film so far has been *Avatar*. The film is 40% live action and 60% computer special effects.

The actors wore special suits that captured their movements. Computer special effects were added later to give the actors their alien looks.

WOW! facts

Avatar is one of the most expensive films ever made. It cost more than £150 million to make.

Aliens continue to be popular with cinema audiences.

The new Star Wars, Marvel and DC comic book films will make sure that we will see many more different types of alien soon.

What do you think these new aliens will look like?

Questions

What is a Goldilocks planet? *(page 6)*

What year was the first Superman film released? *(page 14)*

Who played Spock in the Star Trek TV series? *(page 16)*

What does TARDIS stand for? *(page 23)*

What year was *E.T. the Extra-Terrestrial* released? *(page 27)*

How much money was spent making *Avatar*? *(page 29)*

INDEX

A Trip to the Moon 7
Albert Einstein 28
Batman 15
Chewbacca 19
Drax the Destroyer 13
Easter Island 5
E.T. the Extra-Terrestrial 27
galaxy 22
Gamora 13
Goldilocks planets 6
Groot 13
Guardians of the Galaxy 13
Han Solo 18, 19, 20, 22
Jabba the Hutt 20
Klingons 21
Little Shop of Horrors 11
Nazca desert 5
puppet 24, 25
Rancor 20
sci-fi films 8
spaceships 21, 26
Star Trek 16, 21, 31
Star Wars 18-19, 24, 30
Steven Spielberg 26
Superman 14-15, 31
Tardis 23
The War of the Worlds 9
The Blob 10
This Island Earth 10
The Iron Giant 12

universe 6
Vin Diesel 12
White House 22
Yoda 19, 24